Copyright

First published in Great Britain 1998 by I.C.C.S.

140 Tabernacle Street, Suite 3.1, London EC2A 4SD

Telephone Number 0171 336 6197

Fax 0171 251 9384

All artwork and typeset created by Jason Dinsdale

Printed by

Hillary Press Ltd
75 Church Road
London NW4 4DP

REVISITING the BATTLEGROUND

(Experience of abuse within the Church)

Foreword by Richard Chartres
The Bishop of London

by Jez Bevan Todd

Acknowledgements

For Malcolm and Rosemary,

with thanks for continual

love and acceptance.

Much thanks also, to all those who allowed me to look beyond my pain.

Foreword from the Bishop of London

I first met Jez Todd when he was working for an addiction recovery project in the East End. I was impressed by the speed with which he seemed able to win the confidence of a wide variety of people. He was also able to meet them at their points of pain and vulnerability. After reading this moving book, I begin to understand some of the reasons for this ability.

I then discovered that Jez had completed his training for Ordination, yet not been Ordained. His book also reveals some of his ambivalence about the institutional church. Although it may be unfashionable to say so, institutional structures are essential for translating the moral and spiritual imaginations of individuals into a shared vision in a form that can have an impact on the way we live together. But every church also needs people to work on the frontiers, skirmishing and exploring relatively unencumbered by institutional lumber. The Church of England would be wise to make more provision for such people among the ranks of its full time leaders. Although Jez is now ordained, he works within the context of a visionary local church in front line missionary work and community building.

I commend this book to you as the first few chapters of a life which is still unfolding. Some religious practice contains a large admixture of ego projection and wish fulfillment. It takes time and frequently pain to come home to the Father of Our Lord Jesus Christ who is beyond our manipulation and who is not confined by our definitions. This book is a hopeful account of the early stages of a sometimes painful journey into a deep and adventurous faith in the only God who is; the God who is not the confection of our fear or fantasy; the God who makes Himself known in the life, death and resurrection of Jesus Christ.

+Richard Londin:

The Rt. Revd. and Rt. Hon. R.J.C. Chartres

INDEX

Prologue. 'The Challenge'

I remember a conversation I had with a Muslim psychiatric patient, at a London hospital where I worked as a chaplain. As we sat talking about his health and belief, he suddenly commented that as people we spend much of our time chasing after material possessions and security. His comment was that none of us ever really choose to chase after spirituality, which he considered much more important.

Apart from yet another profound insight coming from those on the edge of our society, it was a personal challenge to me. I had spent a long time chasing my own anger and pain. It was a familiar struggle, and one which had denied me growth and life. The chase had now became exhausting.

My reality during this time was simply an awareness of my own pain. It was my story. The only one I really knew how to tell. My challenge came though within the possibility that the story was not yet finished. Pain may just be a part of the experience, rather than a constant reality.

This is a story in which abuse is evident, but I do not want the word to simply become sexually associated. As will become evident from this story, sexual abuse occurs primarily because there has already been a wider abuse of power.
The abused then already know vulnerability and alienation.

This is not a book about who abusers are, so much as why these situations emerge. In a general sense life can be abusive. This may indeed be a neccessary insight as we look to the journey ahead.

Thomas Merton a famous Monk of this century wrote:
"There is no greater disaster in the spiritual life than to be immersed in unreality".

This then is the challenge...

Chapter 1: 'Shattered Dreams'

"Darling, could you wait a minute before going to school." These were the words spoken by Mum, which were to create a catalyst of events of a devastating nature. I was waiting in the hall, school bag in hand as she added;

"Your Father will not be going to work for a while."

"Why not?" I exclaimed.

Mum gently told me that he was having to go into hospital for some tests.

"He will be going back to work won't he?"

"Yes," replied Mum. "This is only temporary so that he can get better again."

I was vaguely aware that Dad had been unwell, as the previous summer we had been asked to be quiet as Dad was off work and needed to rest. No explanation was given, it simply was, fact.

I was twelve at the time with lots of expectations and aspirations for life, now I was suddenly being told that Dad would not be going to work, as he was unwell. This was a complete bolt from the blue, all I can remember was an immediate pain. I clung to Mum's reassurance as all that I required, not wanting to consider what to tell my friends, my teacher; or to think of the implications for myself.

I faced the news with a child's optimism, believing that everything must turn out all right. My mind returned to the events of the present, and I walked towards the door for my trip to school. As the door shut I was unaware that this was to be the end of my childhood.

I had up until this point not really experienced any type of pain. My home was a friendly and open place, and I had a family who doted on me as the youngest, and only son. We were a close family and always went away together, holidays were spent at Nana's, roaming free on the Welsh mountainside. There was no reason for any of this to change; I was still young and felt entitled to this continuing lifestyle of stability and love.

What began as sick leave for Dad emerged as medical retirement after six months, and life seemed to issue its first betrayal. Dad was admitted to hospital for neurological tests, but no diagnosis was found; he then became the man who was sick with no illness.

It was at this point that I shed my first tears of despair, as it shouldn't have turned out like this. What had initially begun as a hiccup in the course of events, was now establishing itself as a constant reality.

I began to ask myself, what I would tell my friends? It was an age when everyone was just becoming conscious of parents' jobs and status. I could now tell them nothing, as it was 'nothing' that my Dad did. I was only vaguely aware that he had been a Doctor, but none of this mattered anymore as a Doctor without a practice was of no consequence.

I think I even made things up of a vague nature such as, 'He's in business', or 'He works for the Post Office', or the ultimate; 'It's too complicated to explain.' It's ironic that in the ambiguity of the last comment most truth was to be found.

I was beginning to discover at this early age that there are no absolute role models. Both parents don't have to work, one can be ill while the other one stays at home to look after him. I began to separate my family life, consequently school and Church took on completely different identities. As a result I became increasingly unhappy, and developed a cutting sarcasm; in an attempt to keep people at a distance. This sarcastic response to friends, established my strict boundaries between school, Church and home life. Nobody, including myself, knew of my true pain and confusion, as I did not allow anyone near me.

Dad was reluctantly beginning to see the Doctor more frequently, as Mum pressurised him towards some form of self-help. In these initial stages it was thought that Dad was developing Parkinson's Disease; as he was having some trouble with walking, and there were the beginnings of Parkinsonian facial expression. Throughout the rest of his life Dad was to experience his own questions alongside those of others, as to his diagnosis. As a family we never knew how much personal analysis preoccupied Dad .

It was an ironic fact that Dad was a Doctor, possessing more insight into the possibilities of the illness then we had. He had spent his previous job as a Consultant in Occupational Health with the task of assessing people's fitness for work. It was then for us, his family, devastatingly tragic that he should now exchange roles, in this awful scenario.

Up until primary school, Dad had shown a keen interest in all of my academic and social activities. He had followed me to football matches and stood behind the goal talking to me, encouraging me to dive at the attackers legs! We shared much in sport and school. I respected and loved him, and there was never a point in which I felt disappointed in my parents.

My home was an open and friendly place. We were always encouraged to bring friends home, and having four sisters this generally meant that the house was always occupied by someone. There was a strong sense of togetherness within the family, with little rivalry.

My parents had always attended church and their roles were typical of many; Mum made the coffee, and Dad was a sidesman. Mum and Dad had always attended this church, and had been there for about 15 years by my early teens. As children we had attended the youth groups and enjoyed the social activities, never regarding attendance as a negative requirement. When we reached the age of 12 our parents considered us old enough to make up our own minds, as to whether or not we wanted to attend church. When I reached this momentous age I just continued to go. I was unaware of a conscious decision, but know I just had an awareness of God within an environment that I found safe and comfortable.

During my early teens a new vicar arrived. I was too young to fully appreciate the series of events, but I do recall a substantial change to a more charismatic emphasis. The choir was disbanded, hymn books were exchanged for choruses and a more informal chatty style developed. It was nice as the Church family became more familiar, and the services became more hi-tec in presentation. As this period progressed we moved into a charismatic emphasis which involved loud vocal expressions of praise, and a more intimate approach to God. People began to talk about the miracles they experienced in their lives. Everything was new and exciting as we

entered into unknown territory in pursuit of the Holy Spirit. I just sat and listened with great excitement as God was made more real to me.
John Wimber, an American evangelist was invited to teach us all about the Power of the Holy Spirit. He spoke about how God wanted to heal people **now** from all sorts of ailments. We were told that Pentecost was again within our grasp; all that was required was a baptism of the Holy Spirit. To become empowered to minister as the disciples first did. This visit from John Wimber was to change the whole direction of the Church, as people fed on this teaching. It was as if an electric charge went around the congregation; and we all waited eagerly to be switched on.

Despite levels of ambiguity and confusion, it was with a general enthusiasm that I greeted the charismatic approach; although I did possess some questions. I wanted to ask why certain people met God in such a powerful way and others did not? Why was any previous faith I held, now defunct in comparison with this new one? It was a period when conversion was having to be qualified, and first and second class citizenship developed. There was a division between those who had been 'touched' or 'blessed' and the rest of us who remained interested or reluctant observers. Slowly what might be called a 'leper' scenario began to develop. It felt at times so isolating to be part of a group, and yet slightly excluded because of others 'Experience'. There was much pain and confusion as I and many others had to question the validity of our faith, in terms of whether we had the latest spiritual gift or experience.

I remember the first challenge to this approach had developed within a facetious remark relayed by Dad, as we sat together in a service. Somebody had stood up and said that they believed that there was a person in the congregation who had a headache, whom God wanted to heal. My Dad had then turned around to me and said that he would bring a packet of aspirins to next week's service, as it would make a lot of people very happy!

This slightly cynical approach from a trained Doctor provoked in me a series of questions as to the validity of the 'word' shared. I began to consider why God would want to heal someone of something for which we already had a cure? As I began to pursue this line of thought with my Church elders, I was told that the headache itself was not especially significant, it was simply an indication that God cared for that person and wanted to heal them of some emotional trauma which was of far greater significance. The physical symptom/ailment was then a "secondary external expression symbolising a primary emotional concern". Well, it was confusing enough to convince me.

Gradually however as this style of ministry developed in the Church, it became less like Russell Grant's question time, and was more specific in nature. Eventually actual medical conditions were given and the healing ministry was unleashed, with the claim that God wants everyone healed now.

It was these words that I had been waiting to hear. Healing was now said to be the prerogative of any person who had enough faith. Everything was now going to be all right, it was just a question of time. I had not really considered my Dad's condition in relation to the Church, until the charismatic movement introduced its theology of healing. Now I began to believe that when the Bible spoke of Jesus binding up the broken hearted, it was really meant for me. Jesus could and would heal my Dad. If only I took him to the right meeting, then our lives would return to normal.

My Dad had been medically retired for just over a year, and I was fourteen years old when I began my mission for his health. I did not tell my friends at school about what was happening. I kept the mission strictly Church centred. After all the church claimed to hold all the answers.

Adolescence is often a period of insecurity and confusion, as one enters a transition period; of trying to establish yourself in the adult world. These were certainly my feelings, which were coupled with the added burden of desperately wanting to make everything all right again. On occasions I felt like a small child who was lost and confused, wandering around in a daze. I did not even know the right questions to ask. I simply wanted somebody to listen and explain it all to me. It was then extremely hard to build up the courage to ask a Church leader to visit my Dad. I remember a youth meeting in which I spoke to someone for the first time.

“What's the matter Jeremy?”

“Well, it's my Dad, He's not very well.”

“What's the matter with him?”

“I don't really know.”

“What would you like me to do?”

“Well, I want him to get better and be healed.”

I must have spoken these words to so many. I felt stupid and repetitive, but I just wanted the situation to get better and for everything to return to normal. I would have done anything to make this happen.

I was not prepared for the response to my painful situation, I received from some of the adults to whom I spoke. Often a conversation would ensue involving me attempting to explain my heartache, I would then be asked, "Does your father really want to get well?" As I exclaimed Yes, they asked; "Why does he not then go to their healing services?" Since my reply was always that he preferred a quieter form of worship. The adult's belief was always inevitably that my Dad was not open.

This response added to the pain I already felt as I was forced to question my Dad's own faith, in relation to which services he attended. I was bursting to say, ‘but he believes’ this though was thrown into doubt as his credentials were assessed. I was asked to encourage him to attend some of the more charismatic meetings, as this was where I was told God would meet him. This was then my task and I pursued it vigorously in my attempt to find a cure.

On occasions, I felt as if Dad had in some way betrayed me. It was an almost apologetic boy who approached church elders with the request that they do something about his Dad's illness. Some months later my perseverance and persuasive tongue eventually got a response from the leadership to our family's plight.

There was a ring on the bell and I opened the door to a group of church leaders. The Curate and a few respected members of the ministry team crowded into our front living room. This was unexpected and unannounced, but my heart was racing as this was the moment for which I had been waiting. The occasion when God would reach out and heal my Dad; so that he could return to work and everything would be normal again. I was asked to leave the room while the team gathered around Dad to lay hands on him and anoint him with oil.

When the last person had left I bounded in with great expectation. I met a rather tired set of parents who wanted to know why these people had come. They had been embarrassed and uncertain as to the purpose of this unannounced visit. I was told afterwards that about five people had gathered around Dad placing their hands on him while praying. Later on he had been anointed with oil and the specific prayer for healing had been made. After it was all over Dad had been asked if he'd felt anything happen, he replied no, and everyone left. (In fact this was not simply a departure from this meeting, but a departure from our lives for another

four years, during which time Dad became progressively worse.)
I was devastated that nothing had happened during this special service. Why had God not healed him or even given some encouragement during this time? It had all seemed so easy. You went to God and asked for his healing power, he gave it to you and everyone would praise him for ever and ever, Amen. Unfortunately, it didn't happen like this for us. We were unable to give testimony along with the others at the next healing service. We were left to pick up the pieces of a very embarrassing and crushing experience.

I didn't really speak about the incident with my parents at this point. I was simply asked not to involve other people in my parents affairs without permission.

For me however the struggle to understand continued. Why had the formula not worked? Why had Dad not been healed? In my mind at this time, there could only be two solutions: Either Dad did not truly believe or God did not care. Both solutions were too dreadful for me to consciously accept.

I took my questions to my youth leaders.

"Why was he not healed?" I enquired.

"Well I'm not sure. Do you know what happened?"

"No, not exactly."

I felt like a child who had asked the wrong question to an adult who knew the answer but was reluctant to give it. The next question said it all.

"Does he actually want to be healed?"

Now the responsibility was shifted away from the 'carers' to the sufferer. It was Dad's faith level which was assessed, and the yardstick was his lack of healing.

During these early years of adolescence I was pulled strongly in two directions. One was the desire to enter more fully into the charismatic movement as it offered me blind hope. The other was to believe firmly that my parents were both Christians and to accept that I didn't know the reasons for Dad's suffering. I juggled around with these issues for a long time, and became confined to the periphery of indecision. I do not think that it was until the last two years of my Dad's illness, that I ever firmly believed again that they were both Christians; because of this appalling formula I had been fed. In fact during this time I often prayed for my parents conversion; if only they could just attend a few of the right meetings and learn the new teaching. I knew that they possessed a faith, but I was being told that it was not dynamic enough. If it had been Dad would have received healing by now.

I was fifteen when my period of disenchantment began to fully emerge. I noticed a lady in the congregation who had Multiple Sclerosis. She had always been there and was surely a prime candidate for any healing which God might wish to bestow. I began to see the expectation and then the pain on the faces of visitors, as we all waited desperately during the 'words of knowledge'; praying that it would be us that God had mercy on. There was so much power in the preachers voice. I really believed he knew the heart of God. It was a strange time, as I always wanted to be 'blessed' though was always rather sceptical about it. I desperately wanted to be released from my questions, but they always remained rooted in reality.

When I was sixteen Dad was beginning to show noticeable signs of deterioration. On the occasion of my sisters engagement party he fell as we were leaving. He quickly turned around to those there and made a joke about having drunk too much. The painful realisation of Dad's loss of equilibrium was disguised in an alcoholic joke from a man who didn't drink. My form teacher had commented that Dad had noticeably deteriorated since he had last seen him; I felt like screaming at my teacher. "I don't want to be told that my Dad is getting worse'.

Theories were flying around; could it be Parkinson's, Multiple Sclerosis, Motor Neurone? Why did no-one know, and why were we all so powerless to help him?

I think in retrospect I was unaware to the extent of confusion I was feeling. I was desperate for answers. The medical practitioners could offer no insight. I was left with my faith on which I would once again pin all my hopes. I knew 'healing' hadn't worked before but now I had read more books, I felt more mature and that I possessed a faith and love which could overcome all obstacles.

So I returned once more to the people I perceived could bring healing. To those whose rallying cry was, 'We will bind up the broken hearts'. Why should I have looked anywhere else?

The time came when people began to tell me that my struggling had to stop, that I should let God be God, and begin to trust him with all of my fears. I remember desperately wanting to believe and hearing Alan, a youth leader and friend, tell me how he believed God would heal him of a deformed arm. If Alan could believe this in his own life, then I too would believe this for Dad. I am writing over ten years later and Alan's arm has not been healed.

One day I entered Dad's room he was lying on his bed reading.

"Dad I've got something I want to tell you. I know that it has been extremely hard for you recently, but I believe that God will heal you."

As he listened to me he said nothing. I don't even remember if I stayed after I'd told him this; but I just wanted him to know. Like any zealous convert I felt I had done my duty and expressed my faith, in the hope that it would encourage him.

I was still listening to very emotive charismatic claims, charged with hope and expectation; praying fervently that God would hear my prayer, so that Dad might be the next to stand before the congregation and give his testimony as to God's healing power. It was as if I was just waiting for our turn, as the speaker interviewed yet another cured person. I was of course happy for them, but only in the context of anticipating our moment of glory.

There would be little integrity if I did not acknowledge that some healing did occur. I did see people released from emotional turmoil on many occasions. There was deep healing which occurred in peoples memories; others received physical cures from all types of ailments. I knew a lady who had been cured of cancer through prayer. There was also a close friend of mine who had been prayed for and been cured of very bad asthma. I have no desire to limit or rubbish the possibility of God's activity through healing. It is because I believe in healing, that it has become so important to distinguish the fact from the fiction.

I feel though that much of what was claimed as healing during this time was simply people rediscovering the power of being listened too and valued, for I am convinced that these remain the great gifts God has given us.

Sadly however I observed an unhealthy separation developing between the unwell and the well. I saw the expectation of all who suffered, and I wanted there to be more recognition of their plight. I didn't believe they could change their situation if only they possessed enough faith, they could not cure themselves. They needed somebody to be there for them, someone to understand, someone who could speak of their own fear and need. Unfortunately there appeared to be an even greater sense of fear amongst those who were well, than those who were suffering.

I continued to pray for healing for Dad, but felt by this time that it must come in a more personal, less dramatic way. God could work discretely or with great signs of power. I was not to choose the method, just simply pray for the result. Now my energies began to be totally channelled into finding meaning for his life; for in this way I too would be healed of the deep pain that engulfed me.

Despite the previously singular spiritual focus, I now began focusing on the practical aspects of life. I looked for relevant jobs Dad could do; and was again asking anyone within the church if they had any ideas and suggestions. I did not want Dad to just become a man who was identified by the label of his illness.

He was a man who desperately needed the recognition of his whole humanity.

Chapter 2: Betrayed

One of the difficulties I have had in adult life has been in not being able to fully articulate my entire experience as a teenager. People had become very familiar with the story about Dad's pain. It was a story I told well and within which I was totally immersed. It was only when somebody once commented to me during an interview, that they knew the impact of my Dad upon my life, but wanted to know: What was my personal story? Perhaps it's true to say that much of my adult life has sought to respond to this question; in an attempt to understand and resolve this turbulent period.

When I was fifteen and at the height of my isolation through my Dad's illness, I became good friends with a church youth leader. It was a friendship which naturally developed out of us working together at the church youth group; and a relationship I quickly came to value. It would be true to say that this person Chris, was the only person who I felt was consistently concerned with how I was feeling.

Amongst the pain and heartache however, I had also found friendship with a girl who I knew from church and school. It was, I suppose, typical of many teenage relationships, except for the intensity. We would spend a lot of time together, walking in the rain, coming home late and generally behaving like teenagers do.

The relationship began to go wrong, when I think we both began to glimpse the huge emotional burdens that we carried. She was hurting and in need of love, and therefore made me her entire focus. I don't think for a minute that this was because I was the nicest boy she'd met to date, but probably had more to do with our pain.

Well it doesn't take a psychologist to point out that the burdens we carried were too great at this juncture, and we became exhausting for each other. Neither one of us could properly care for the other, as we were having difficulty adequately caring for ourselves. After some time I could no longer deal with the situation so ended the relationship. There were some tears but we were only fifteen. I naturally supposed that the episode was over, and sank back into my own melancholy. Never imagining the train of events that were about to unfold, and which would almost destroy me.

I remember one day being asked to go and see Alan the main church youth leader; who had until this point been a good and trusted friend. He was a man in his late thirties who had always been considerate and caring. As I entered his home I was immediately aware that this was not an informal visit, but something more serious.

I do not even remember if I sat down, before the question was launched at me. ARE YOU GAY? Well it didn't even evolve after some social chit chat, it wasn't even subtle. There were no tea and biscuits, just the words: Are YOU gay? At first I was dumbfounded as I had no opinion as to what it was to be gay.
It was my first encounter with homophobia, and it was as unacceptable then as it is now. This was a powerful and traumatic accusation, levelled at an already confused and bewildered boy.

My first response was to ask what this was all about, I then became angry. I was told that some people had been concerned about how much time I had been spending with my friend Chris. It was suggested that I might be in a gay relationship. It was all a bit baffling as I was only fifteen and Chris was in his twenties. Surely I thought, they should have been asking him and not me. I remember how angry I was, as I wanted to know from where the accusation had emerged. Eventually I was told that my previous girlfriend had been 'concerned' about it.

It wasn't a long walk from Alan's house to where Chris lived. I remember storming out of Alan's house in a fit of pain and confusion. I marched up to where Chris lived. I think on this occasion the 'Hello mate, How's it going?' were neatly side-stepped, as I hurled myself into Chris's room in a state of anger and accusation. If you place two men in a small room and then add the ingredient that one of them was about to explode; you might be able to experience the intensity of emotion. It was no longer a comfortable place. The familiar had been replaced with animosity and mis-understanding.

The great cost of this accusation was borne by Chris and I. The irony was that Chris had in fact told me some time previously that he was gay; and it was of little consequence. I was unaware though of the long lasting devastation that this accusation would impose on our friendship. It was to be two years before we could regain a place of love and friendship.

At first we met to try and understand the true root of all that was being said. We had already spoken about Chris's sexual orientation, but now it became messy. I could not avoid those 'caring' murmuring voices which surrounded me at church, and found their way to school in the less subtle language of playground taunts.

I was so angry much of the time that I mis-directed my anger onto Chris.

Deep within I knew that Chris was the only adult person who really cared about all that was happening to me at home. This love and commitment was now removed for a time, as his friendship was being taken from me through other peoples prejudice and hang-ups.

It was an extremely painful time for Chris as he ended up leaving the church. Like so many other gay people, he knew the intolerance towards his remaining.

I have to say that I've never understood why this accusation was launched at me, without my parents first being told. Indeed Chris, as an adult was accused but not confronted. It was typical of my experience of life in that place. I experienced the full impact alone.

The developing rumours at my School and in the church that I was gay, added to my confusion as I tried to understand what was happening to me. The snide remarks and undercurrents were so difficult to take. I became paranoid at this stage, and found little comfort in the friends with whom I had grown up. On occassions it was simply another offensive remark levelled at me by those who did not like me. The accusation though possessed so much power, because I was beginning to wonder if it was true.

I don't remember talking to any friends about how I was feeling, as I was scared that this would heighten the rumour making and make absolute my isolation. My greatest concern until this point had been to separate my home life from all other activities and encounter. I needed my pain to be anonymous before others. Home was now not a place to bring friends to. Not because they were not welcome; but because the harsh reality of our family life may have been too much for them.

Life became increasingly worse, as the personal rumours and accusations developed. Initially I would ignore these, and manage to maintain my role in the teenage group of which I was a part. Though I probably could not say that I belonged at this point, as my group place was becoming increasingly vulnerable. The personal fear of rejection from my peer group led me to distance myself. I would stand in the school dinner queue and listen to the beginning of snide and sarcastic comment, not vicious expressions, just words charged with innuendo and challenge. The worst aspect of all of this was the fact that I could not talk to any of my friends about the rumours, as it would have been seen by some as an admission of guilt.

The only time that I was ever directly confronted about my sexuality was on a youth camp, which my previous girlfriend attended. In the escapism of a weeks holiday, complete strangers would approach me with comments of derision and fun. It was not the fact that I was being called queer which really bothered me; it was simply that a rumour followed me into all aspects of my private life.

The result was a period of withdrawal from all stratas of life, the church was now a place which not only accused my Dad, but me also. My parents became so increasingly concerned about my depressive moods, that they decided to go and see the church leader, about the rumours of which their daughter was allegedly a part.

I felt terrible, as I knew how hard it was for them to do this. My Dad was an increasingly sick man who was losing confidence rapidly. Now it was necessary for him to return to the man who had prayed for his healing, and never returned. It was an awful situation and one which I felt terribly guilty about.

When my parents returned, I did not bound in with any expectation. I do not even remember if I even saw them that evening. All that was said when we did speak about it, was that the parents could not believe that their daughter would be involved in rumours like these. So the situation was left unfinished, the church shutters had come down. We as a family were left once again with our own pain, enhanced by the judgement and accusation of the institution.

I have no doubt that this was not a brilliant sequence of events for me personally. In fact if I am to be a touch honest I'd say that the church did not endear itself to me. Indeed the church, the place which had once been familiar, was becoming increasingly alien. I used to sit in the church lounge after the morning service surrounded by my contemporaries and their 'holy' parents. I was confused and wanted desperately to belong to this group which had once been so familiar. I am not certain as to why I even stayed with this church, except to say that desperation and exhaustion had taken their toll. To leave another structure which had previously been so important, remained simply too terrifying. Anyway it was my local church, and I couldn't drive.

Six months passed and in this time I learnt the important skill of detachment. How to be a part of a group but not belong to it. Family life was frighteningly consistent, with fear and anxiety ruling the day.

Events were to change though when within one particular church service a request was made. There was to be a large conference hosted by the church for a week, families in the parish were asked to consider hosting clergy.

Chapter 3: 'A Priest and a Bishop'

It was something of a shock to us children when our parents told us that we were to receive a priest and a Bishop to stay. Our family had never done anything like this before. I was not sure why my parents had decided to host these clergy, in retrospect I think possibly they may in some way have been trying to reconcile themselves to the church.

Two men arrived, a Canadian Bishop and a Priest from Papua New Guinea. They were a friendly pair and appeared to fit in well with the family. Bishop Chuck was a càring man whose wife was suffering from Parkinson's disease. Mum subsequently discovered a comforting and sympathetic ear. The Priest Bill was also a friendly man who had noticed my depression, and took time to talk to talk to Mum and Dad about their son. My parents subsequently told him all about the accusations I was experiencing as well as the pain of Dad's illness.

Initially Bill would come to talk with me about how I was, he would speak with me of God and offer general concern. I was a little confused by this attention; but was grateful to anyone who could acknowledge my pain. During this time there were incidents with which I felt uncomfortable. I was weight training a lot and generally keeping fit. Bill used to show great interest in this, and would often come and weight train with me and a friend. He was on occasion touchy. I was simply aware that there was some aspect to his person which made me uncomfortable.

It seems almost naive as an adult writing now, but then 99% of any abuse is instigated by somebody who has gained trust. I was often unsure how to respond to this man who was a guest in our home, and also a priest. At this stage I chose to perceive his hugs and physicality to be a sign of his Christian love and affection.

One particular evening however when I had gone to bed there was a knock at my bedroom door. Bill entered saying he wanted to say goodnight to me. I was somewhat shocked at his presence, but couldn't say anything. Bill then came towards me as if to hug me. I felt extremely confused by this as he held me very tightly and touched my genitals and kissed me. I pushed him away. It is difficult to know what else to write as nothing else happened, except I was kissed and groped by a priest.

Another knock came on the door and my twin sister Penny walked in. This may have been the only time when she experienced a twin's premonition. As Penny entered the room she saw us in an embrace. Bill quickly retorted that we had been praying, and briskly left. I do not remember ever speaking to Penny about this incident at the time. I think it remained for all of us an unspeakable moment of confusion and fantasy. Neither do I remember speaking about the event to anyone in the subsequent days. All I remember is that when Bill was leaving, I was told off for my reluctance in coming to say goodbye.

I must be honest about this whole episode and say that I was not sure what had gone on. Sexual abuse doesn't really register the first time. It is simply just another experience. Something not wanted and not willingly entered into. Eventually though even this became the subject of considerable personal scrutiny. It is difficult when you're fifteen and have been accused of all sorts of sexual allegations, not to eventually wonder if you have not brought the entire situation upon yourself.

It is even more difficult when you are already suffering so much pain. I did not talk to my parents or anyone about the assault for considerable time. Mainly because I had nothing to say. After all what comments are appropriate from a fifteen year old boy about a priest who had been a guest in your family home?

This however was not to be the end of the story. As in the first experience Bill was to initiate contact with me, forcing me to acknowledge at least something of what had occurred.

I used to work in a paper shop. I was a part of the young Thatcher generation who really knew how to work. You know the sort of industrious teenager, I was the one who had two paper rounds and any extras on Saturdays. I never volunteered on a Sunday, not through religious motivation but because the papers were always far too heavy. I had though left these back breaking exploits to everyone else and had worked my way up from paper rounds to the heady heights of a marker up. What this really meant was that I was stupid enough to get up at five o'clock every morning for more money.

One morning the owner of the shop came in and said there was a parcel for me. I was extremely surprised as there was no reason to be receiving mail at this address. I opened it quickly and found inside a shirt, a book on God's love, some money and a letter from Bill. I was extremely embarrassed and ashamed. I immediately thought that everybody would know what had happened and start accusing me again of being gay. I quickly shoved the letter back inside the wrapping and waited until I returned home.

As I opened the front door I hurriedly went to my bedroom. Despite what had happened here I still felt that it was a safe and secure place. It was here that I began to read what was a pornographic letter, with Bill expressing his sexual fantasy about me.

Bill had in fact written to me before and was enquiring as to why I had not replied. He had wanted me to go and visit him, as he had taken accommodation not far from where I lived. My initial reaction was one of fear and confusion. I felt ashamed about the letter. In it Bill spoke of love and something special that we shared. I wanted to scream at him, to kick and punch him, to make him know that he was not welcome in my life. But Bill was a Priest.

I was an angry boy caught in the pain of life, unable to articulate clearly the frustration and upset I was feeling. I did not know how to argue with a man who had been a guest in our home. I was not clever enough to see the perversion and twisted nature of his expression of God's love. I was in a place of total conflict as his words of 'love', were met with my fierce anger. I did not know what was right or wrong, as Bill sought to implicate and draw me into his fantasy.

It was possibly this loss of control and choice which was one of the hardest things with which to deal. It was the not knowing if I had in some way brought this upon myself. All I had to go on in terms of the church was that they had told me that I was in a gay relationship. I had denied it and now had another church leader, who knew something of my story, also tell me that I wanted his sexual attention. It really was quite devastating as Bill's words simply compounded with the previous accusations. I had until this point felt I knew who I was; now I was becoming increasingly unclear.

As I sat on my bed crying, my Mum came in. She asked what was the matter and I just said; 'Why didn't you tell me?' In this letter Bill had indicated that he'd written many times to the family home but there had been no reply. He had then remembered that I worked at the paper shop so sent the package there. My Mum just burst into tears and said 'We didn't want you to find out. We were trying to protect you.'

What had in fact happened was that an elder sister Jane, had been suspicious of Bill's response to me. Being of a genuinely interfering, if not protective nature, she decided to open a letter that he sent me after his departure. The letter was to be the beginning of a stream of pornographic mail, in which the priest expressed his fantasies and sexual desire. Jane had been outraged and wrote back demanding that the communication stop. There had been a subsequent discussion with my parents, and they had decided that I had experienced enough. They tried to protect me from this man, despite their ignorance at this stage as to the actual sexual assault.

It was then while sitting on the bed in my bedroom, that I told my Mum something of what had happened. We simply held each other and cried.

Unknown to me during this recent period my parents difficulty had developed beyond their initial visit to the curate. They were aware of the developing rumours which were spread about me. Just as neighbours and church members were aware of some speculation as to my sexual orientation. I can remember one evening when I was asked by Mum and Dad if I could speak with them. It was rather formal, but I obliged. It was a time in which Mum and Dad offered me an acceptance, which would become the most precious gift I had ever received from them.

'Jeremy', my Dad began.

'I want you to know that it makes no difference to me what your sexuality is. You are always my son, and I will continually love and support you.'
In this acceptance I was able to tell my Dad what had actually happened to me. He then made the painful decision to once again return to the local clergy to tell them of this trauma. I do not know what went through my Dad's mind, as he reconciled himself to the thought of seeing the local clergy again. It must have been a very distressing experience for a man who was already suffering increased personal pain.

On his return, Dad simply said that he had spoken to the Vicar, but was told that there was really little that could be done. The priest Bill would be written to and told to leave me alone, he would also be unwelcome in the parish. It was the final comment though which was to offer the real betrayal. I listened as Dad told me that the Vicar had allegedly said, that it would be best not to pursue this situation as it would cause adverse publicity and damage to the man's reputation and this local church.

I can not describe what feelings I had, because I was once again numb, believing that I had made a fuss about nothing. It was a time of great sexual confusion. There were continuous rumours circulating about me, and I continued to question whether in fact they were true. Why was it that I was receiving all this attention from men? Maybe I in some way asked for it? Much of the pain that I felt during this time was not only to do with a developing questioning of my sexuality. It was about not being believed.

I wanted to scream out at people,
"DON'T YOU UNDERSTAND. IT REALLY HURTS. I WANT SOMEBODY TO EXPLAIN ALL OF THIS TO ME."

I was desperate for support, and I clung to the church like a wounded animal who needed the pack. This was despite my being unsure if the church might turn on me once again and destroy me.

I found it difficult to sleep, and was having continual disturbing sexual images of Christ on the cross. These were pictures which I was ashamed and embarrassed about. I had no control of them and just wanted them out of my head. It got to such a stage that I decided the only way to try and resolve them, was to once again see the curate. As an adult this appears a crazy and naive idea, to return to a man who had caused so much pain. I believed though that if I could sort all of this out then maybe other areas in my life would return to normal.

I can remember feeling very frightened and anxious as I waited outside of the Curate's gate. I felt stupid and ashamed, I did not know how to tell a priest about my perverted sexual dreams of his God. As I knocked on the door, I waited desperately wanting to be embraced and welcomed by this cleric. As the door opened I was ushered into the man's study and asked the reason for my visit.

I don't even remember if I sat down, and certainly can't recall what was said to me. It was all so brief and embarrassing. Nothing of value or help was said, as I remember little of the event, except it's briefness and my feeling of isolation. I can not have been in there for more than five to ten minutes, I left with just an increased sense of alienation and rejection. This was my final betrayal from the church, and I decided from this point that I must make active my withdrawal.

Chapter 4: Waiting

I returned home. I had not told anyone I had gone, as I was too ashamed of the reason. It was then just a time of waiting. Waiting for this pain to stop and for my Dad to die. Predictably the pain did not stop, it simply became refocused onto my Dad. I ceased to think about what I had experienced, and only considered the man I loved. It was relatively easy to place my Dad before myself, as I felt his pain more acutely than my own. I just felt screwed up, and simply interpreted this as the pain a grieving son has for his father.

I did not know what to do with my pain. I did not know who to speak too. There was a wall of silence surrounding me, a deep moat which confounded any attempt made to receive love and support from the adults within the church.

Later I did talk to a few friends about what had happened in the sexual assault. It was ironic that their polarised response represented my dilemma. One friend of similar age wanted to smash and harm the 'perverted evil man' who had done this to me. The other gently tried to help me see that I would never receive the response I wanted and needed from the people of whom I was asking. I must admit though to feeling better understood by my first friend.

I still desperately wanted to belong. To be a part of something, anything but the life that now embraced me. My intensity of need isolated me from others, as I think in retrospect I just wanted to be held. To be protected from the tidal wave of change which kept crashing into my life.

I can remember clearly in my late teens becoming steadily obsessed with a girl I knew I could never have. She became an escape, the possibility of love which would never materialise. Such was my fixation and desire to be held that I lost a stone in a week of depressive anticipation as to whether she might actually want to go out with me. As usual the experience was never as good as the expectation. I began to discover that pain often overwhelms intimacy and that ultimately I felt safer on my own, holding my dreams and disintegration.

As I moved into the sixth form at school, things became increasingly meaningless. I began to see through the eyes of someone who suffers. All was superficial except the one whom I loved the most. I was a recluse who only had concerns for home, and how I might help to alleviate the strain. I had no lovers during this time and school friends became increasingly distanced; sharing no knowledge of the extent of pain and confusion I was experiencing.

I would return home at any available moment just to see Dad or to take him out in his car. Just to sit there so that he would know of my love for him; we didn't talk much at this point it was just a period of being. I began to recognise that despite my passion and fervent belief things were not getting better. I thought of all of the changes which had occurred over those last few years. How I had began to take my Dad swimming to give him some exercise. To hold him so that he could float, to congratulate him on widths achieved. It was so bloody outrageous that things were like this. I wanted to be able to go walking and play squash, with a man who would challenge and shape my masculinity. I wanted to be held and not be the holder.

Life over the following two years had involved little change, I maintained a constant vigil for Dad but moved to the periphery of Church life. I felt guilty and threatened, as my life did not fit into the examples which were always being given us. We weren't a loving Christian family who found great joy in praying together or rejoicing in all aspects of our faith. We were a group of individuals torn apart by the prescribed events.

I still clung onto my own personal hope for Dad, but became more disillusioned with the church's acclamations of victory and faith. It became clear to me as a questioning adult that we had not won a victorious life. There was still much pain for all of us, which could not be cured by the fluttering of hands and fervent prayer. As I prepared to leave home it was with mixed emotion. I was desperate to leave the church of which I was a part. I felt guilty and unwanted. I needed to regain the freedom of thought and choice. We were not taught how to question at church, things were to be accepted in the name of faith.

I managed to scrape through my A Levels but decided to take 'a year out' before returning to the ivory towers of academia. I worked alongside a School's worker and quickly formed a strong friendship which enabled me to talk of my pain. It was remarkable that I had not until this point found many adults receptive to my distress.

As I relayed my story to Richard, the school's worker. I became increasingly aware of my anger and the legitimacy of my questions and subsequent pain. I did not have to apologise for my own experience simply because it was outside of the victorious charismatic one. My life was real to me and my family, the events which had shaped it were facts that could not simply be dismissed as unhelpful or cynical. I re-called how no-one had ever stood at the front of church and spoken of how God had not healed them. No testimony was given from the person whose faith endured the relentless onslaught of sickness, suffering and death. Certainly there were the odd questions asked of the devout Christian who never received healing. These though were usually behind closed doors in hushed whispers, often being regarded as a source of embarrassment. No-one offered the thought that suffering and death could be the legitimate options.

My words became angry at the way I had been accused, at the way Dad had been ignored and removed to some back room, where his cries could not be heard so loudly. Why should I be made to feel guilt, why did I have to apologise for my own experience: for the pain, the doubt and confusion?

I watched Richard as I spoke, looking for those tell-tale signs of embarrassment and the 'all-knowing' expression. None came. There was silence after I had finished speaking. After a time Richard spoke and thanked me for what I had shared. It was such a powerful affirmation, I was no longer under threat of accusation; I HAD BEEN BELIEVED. I had felt almost 'dirty' relaying my experience, as if in some way I was betraying people; but I now knew that Richard had seen beyond my anger to the greater reality of pain. Acceptance is a very powerful gesture, this became the beginning of courage given for my own inner convictions.

During this time my Dad became steadily worse. He considered himself irritating and a fraud, and was often in an extreme anxiety state. It was the self-description of fraud which hurt so much. Did he not know that we had no expectations of him. Who was calling him a fraud? It was not us, as we just wanted to see him well.

Maybe it's not too speculative to suggest that it was a combination of his own self-doubt alongside the church to which he belonged. After all was it not them who had told him that all would be healed, if he believed? In this scenario there can be only one guilty party, this being the one who suffers. He could not be cared for by the church, as his sickness undermined their teaching. There could be no loving God if suffering continued, so it was best to remove those who suffered to maintain the theology. Dad was loved so much, but we were unable to reach into the depression that surrounded him. I wept at his self-appraisal, as we would have done anything to resolve the pain and to restore his self-worth.

As the family entered more fully into this dark cloud, I became increasingly aware that if things did not change, my faith would die. I could no longer hold in tension the concept of an all-loving God who could heal if he chose. Why had he not responded to our continual weeping? I cried with the anguish of the Psalmist that he would remove this suffering from us. I began to fast weekly, to offer my entire day as a prayerful reminder to God of the misery which was continuing within our family. I had no more words to offer and few tears left. I was now speechless towards the pain which was establishing itself.

Chapter 5: 'Deterioration until death do us part'

In the New Year I discovered that Dad had experienced a nervous breakdown. It was a depressing day as I knew that this was serious. It was at this point that we decided as a family to be more open about our feelings. Dad spoke with me and apologised for his condition, and for the trouble he felt he was to the family. I was devastated that he would apologise to us for a situation which constantly tormented him, and to which we could not do enough to respond. There was though a real awareness of his regression, and I spent most of my time on the verge of tears. I became increasingly despondent and desperate to discover some formula which would work. Mum could see that I was particularly depressed at this point, and she told me that Dad's illness would not kill him. There would be a cure. It was just a matter of time.

I was still searching for a spiritual answer and spoke with John, an older Christian friend who was a Doctor. I wanted his medical background and experience to integrate into my framework of Christian faith. He told me that at times he was frightened by the intensity with which I pursued my cause. He expressed that I must begin to let go, and allow God, to be God. He told me that he felt God tell him that I must become a Priest to my family. He asked me if I prayed regularly with my parents? I replied no, it was a more personal, individual expression in our home. He suggested that I begin to do this, that they might be more aware of God's love and concern. I was initially sceptical as I didn't know what to say. I had caused enough pain with my previous Christian fervour. Surely the time was now to pursue private prayer.

I continued to pray for our family situation and was aware of Christ interceding for us. I prayed about the priestly role, and began to perceive the urgency of voicing corporate prayer. If my parents knew of my pain and doubts, this would free them to be honest before their God. To enable all of us to meet God together without guilt and shame. I hadn't really considered their own spiritual need, as I was so engrossed in my own. They needed permission to weep and cry out before God; as we all offered God this hopeless situation. I asked my parents if I could pray with them and they said 'yes'. It became an incredibly powerful thing to petition God with those who suffer.

On one occasion, I asked Dad; "How are you feeling?" It was a stupid question, but one which you ask when there seems nothing left to say. "You love me too much", was his reply; "You must not worry so much, I'm not going to die from it."

It was the first time that we had spoken about death together, and though Dad had appeared optimistic, I wondered whether the very fact death was mentioned indicated significant regression. As we both sat in silence and in tears, we considered the pain we had shared over this endless time. For me the hopes and expectations of a father and son met in this moment, as he asked me to begin to let go of my possessive love of him. He was calm as he spoke.

"I've pleaded with God to help me."

It was sort of whispered and my stunned silence was interspersed with my gentle sobs of, "So have I."

Dad spoke of how he repeatedly pleaded with Christ to have mercy on him and bring healing. I just sat and wept, as I had no adequate expression except the tears and silence. As I left him that evening, I realised that I was trying to console a sick man with a comfort I myself needed to receive.

Dad was now to see a Specialist and we all held out great expectation. This surely would bring the healing that God was going to offer. It did not matter how Dad was healed, as long as it occurred. Despite this expectation, nothing was to materialise for another few months. During this time there was an increasing level of deterioration. The anxiety attacks he experienced were terrifying, as there was little you could do to calm his fears.

I remember a car journey which took on the most frightening dimensions. We had just gone on a short local trip of about eight miles, so that I could pick something up from a friend. Mum had asked if I could take Dad to get him out of the house and to provide a change of scenery. Up until this point Dad had remained rooted at home with no desire to go anywhere. We were frightened that eventually he would not want to leave at all, and his home would become his prison.

As I drove slowly along the cul-de-sac towards the main road, Dad began to slump deeper and deeper into his seat. In fact he gave a vivid visual enactment of wanting the earth to swallow him up. It was indeed a truly pathetic sight, as my father pleaded with me to go slower from the already minimum speed of 30 m.p.h. I just sat at the traffic lights as we approached the junction not knowing what to do. I wanted to rush him home to the safety of his bed, but it was an endless journey ahead. Everything became traumatic for him. I just wanted to protect him from the world.

In the late spring Dad was admitted to Queen's Square in London for a neurological scan, and was becoming very anxious about the tests he was to undergo. I did not appreciate the significance of the scan for him as it would be able to tell us whether they would be able to help him or not.

I was to receive a letter later on from Dad, telling me how concerned he was about the results of the tests. I could only experience a little of his fear at this point, as he wrestled with the thought of possible multiple sclerosis.

The results of the scan were inconclusive. Dad was bemused and didn't want to talk about his condition. We were once more thrown into the pit of splendid isolation, as the medical world for the second time had been unable to offer any insight.

Dad began to regress into childlike roles, but was aware of his mental deterioration. In fact, it was this acute awareness which prevented him from ever being relaxed with anyone. He was embarrassed by his inability to present himself in a 'normal' manner.

I had not fully appreciated the number of obstacles which were there for Dad. Any unfamiliar environment or people proved too much, as he experienced on these occasions his acute loss of control. It was only when I saw him in this context outside of his home, that I appreciated the full extent of his illness. I now knew that I would not have the relationship I so desperately wanted with my father. He would not be able to visit me or go away on holiday. The roles were beginning to be reversed, as I realised not only my continuing need of him, but his fundamental dependence on me.

It was a telephone call from my brother-in-law which catapulted the whole family into the depth of Dad's isolation, dependence and despair.

“Hello, it's Scott.”

“Hello mate, how are you?”

“Yeah, I'm all right. Look the reason I'm phoning is because something has happened and you need to come home.”

“What's happened?”

“Look it doesn't really matter now, I’ll tell you when you get here.”

“No, I need to know. Is it anything to do with Dad?”

“Yes, he's had to go into hospital.”

“Why? Is it serious? What's happened?”

“Look, I didn't want to tell you over the phone, but he's taken an overdose; they're not too hopeful that he will recover .... are you OK. Mate? Now don't do anything stupid in travelling home, you may not be in time to see your father.”

I was absolutely stunned, I just stood there after the phone was dead trying to take the news in. After a while I suddenly became animated and walked into the other room to tell some friends what had happened. They were wonderful and offered to drive me home. I refused as I would need my car once I was there. As my friends prayed for me, I had an overwhelming confidence that I would see Dad again, he wouldn't die. I left to tell Richard my boss, what had happened. As I told him fell into his arms sobbing, devastated by the news.

I drove the 90 miles from Peterborough totally numb, unable to assimilate the information I had just received. I do not remember any of the journey. I simply arrived at home to be greeted by my sister Jane who told me not to be too optimistic. Dad had been given virtually no chance of recovery. I told her that Dad would not die and left for the hospital. In retrospect, I recognise Jane's concern for me as she realised that if Dad had died at this point, it would have totally broken and destroyed me. I needed him to live.

I met Mum and she took me to a bed where Dad was wired up to all sorts of tubes and machinery. We were told by the nurse it was a miracle that he was breathing now; but they were unsure if he would make it through the night. I can give no reason but faith, as I was absolutely certain that Dad would not die. I knew I had to talk with him again. God must reach out and save him. Mum and I said the 23rd Psalm, prayed and I told her that it would be all right and later returned home.

It is difficult to comprehend what pain Dad must have felt, the anguish of his heart. The confusion which surrounded him with no offer of a new start. I just wept as I glimpsed something of his isolation, and remembered his feeling of being a burden to the family. Was his neurosis so great that he could not see that he would never be too great a burden for us to bear? The whole situation was surreal as everything took on a chaotic ill-defined nature. The clarity came with Mum's phone call. Dad was going to pull through. I was not surprised as I had not even entertained the concept of death, I possessed an absolute faith for his life in a way that I'd never experienced before. There was no onslaught of pain, we were just numb to the events; life simply took over and we were dragged along in its slipstream.

I went to visit Dad in hospital but found it hard to respond. I had been told.

"HE IS CHRONICALLY DISABLED, HE WON'T GET BETTER BUT WILL JUST DETERIORATE AND DIE."

It hit me so hard. Why was there no change? Why were the tests useless? Why were we given no diagnosis? As I took Dad to the toilet I fully appreciated his total dependence, the reversal of roles was fully established. Before I left the hospital, Dad said to me:

"You haven't told me that God was looking after me, ... but I know he is."

I did not know what to say, but I was overawed that Dad's faith permeated areas where mine was absent. It had needed to exist as a focus for my desperate emotional need. Like a child hallucinating for food in the depth of hunger and sickness, I too had screamed out for the possibility of life amidst the sickness and death.

Faith was a strange phenomena during this time. The faith which had been so prevalent at the time of the overdose, became afterwards in the cold light of day a difficult concept to grasp. I had wanted healing and yet Dad was not going to improve. I felt that the gift God had given us during this period was more time; but ultimately I realised that the twilight years were washing over us.

Dad had begun to attend a psychiatric day centre twice a week. This was to be the first encounter I had with psychiatric illness on a wider scale. It was frightening and disorientating. There was no denying now that Dad was seriously ill, his regression accelerated greatly. Dad was extremely anxious about the group he attended. On the occasions I took him, it was like leaving an only child at school for the first time. He was becoming so child-like and yet was very aware of all that was happening. He was frightened of the people who were particularly disturbed and disliked the locked wards.

At home he was frightened of everything. To turn on a tap was a major source of anxiety, we were also now beginning to carry him up the stairs. It was an awful thing to undress your father for toilet, and leave him for periods of up to half an hour in a most distressed state. The occasions when I had to carry him up the stairs, began with my male ego being fed by my physical show of usefulness and strength. It was though within the first few steps that I realised the fear of my companion, and deeply regretted this necessary exhibition.

To begin full time care at home was only possible because of the enormous effort made by the whole family. My mum and sister's training as nurses proved invaluable, as the family routine changed entirely to become a place of dying for all of us.

Some more test results arrived relating to the overdose and his stay in hospital. These confirmed the previous news that there was no diagnosis and therefore no medical help. I remained devastated and yet Dad said, "I've asked many times to God's help, and I believe He will respond." I was unable to accept the diagnosis, as I was desperate to believe that there would be some hope. Mum spoke to me of the faith she received from me on the night of the overdose, but I was continually aware that my inner resources were running low. It felt like I had nothing left to believe in.

As Dad continued to deteriorate, the family became increasingly unable to respond to each other. We were all extremely scared by the news we had received, and began to retreat into our own created worlds. The one that I occupied at this time was a place of increasing bleakness. Sunrise never materialised as the darkness of doubt and uncertainty took hold. A conference was arranged with the Psychiatrist at the hospital Dad was attending, and the family assembled to listen to what the professionals had to say.

I can only describe this encounter as the day that Dad died. I along with all of my family was told to dismiss all thoughts of hope, the professionals expressed that he wouldn't improve. We were told that deterioration had set in causing irreversible damage; this would continue until death do us part.

As I listened to this learned and vulnerable man try and explain this unacceptable fact to a family desperate for hope, I wanted to scream out, 'BUT I LOVE MY DAD'. It was the naive and pure hope that love would conquer all.

My hope was crushed by the professionals, as we were left to argue over Dad's motives for life or death. I was unable to identify my true emotions as I felt so isolated and unable to respond. I felt very depressed about the overdose as everyone else was calling it a suicide attempt. I needed to feel at this time that it was simply a cry for help.

Until this point no-one beyond the immediate family had really taken Dad completely seriously. His illness was undefined, and therefore the response to him had been limited. I felt his personal thoughts of feeling a fraud were only there because of the subtle accusation by some, that his illness was to some extent his own creation. The overdose was the first real statement Dad had made which forced the attention of the onlookers. Recognition and help would only come if he demanded the hands of Job's comforters.

As I considered the Psychiatrist who had taken a strong interest in my faith, I was aware that if I could not reconcile Dad's pain with it, my faith would be destroyed. Was I simply a naive son who wanted desperately for things to change; or was I right in assessing Dad's overdose as a cry from the heart?

I left the house and began to walk aimlessly around the familiar sites of the town. I passed my old Primary School and thought of my happy childhood. I remembered the plays and sport I had been involved in, of how delighted and proud Mum and Dad had been. Now all hope began to leave me, as I returned home weeping into the arms of Mum. I had travelled a long way since the child reluctantly on his way to school. This child had simply been told that his Dad wouldn't be going to work for a while.

I spoke again with John, my older Christian friend, who told me I should let go and not struggle against things I did not understand. I argued that I had been led to believe that the Church did have understanding in this area. Yet now I had to reaffirm my trust in God, as I was left with nothing else. I was losing this doctrine of absolute faith. I could only concentrate on what I hoped God was like, as the charismatic image I had been given was beginning to shatter.

Chapter 6: 'Murmured Words'

I was now preparing to leave home for a second time to take up a place at an Anglican theological training college, where I would take my degree. This process had been set in place at the end of my A' Level's. Theological training had always felt inevitable; but like many of my friends, I was simply taking a degree in a subject of interest.

In retrospect it is strange to me that when my faith was at it's lowest ebb, I pursued theological training. Some would say that theological colleges are the worst place to be in a spiritual crisis. In other ways it was a relief to be going. A new identity with no-one having knowledge of my home life. I was about to leave a home where every emotion was charged and intense. I knew that once I had gone my practical help would be limited.

All of us were now seeing a man deteriorate before our eyes, and the internal changes we had to make were tremendous. It was the simple but practical things which caused the most upheaval. Dad could no longer go to the toilet on his own, so we had to pull down his trousers and stare at his groin. It was in this situation that I knew the role reversal was complete, I was now helping my father go to toilet just as he had helped me. The only significant difference was that I had not been able to do it on my own as a child. Here was a man of fifty-seven who had to ask for help from his children, in a humiliating scenario.

I cannot imagine what it was like to have your son stare at you completely naked and exposed, and yet be helpless to function without him. I remember an occasion when I told Dad that I would be back to help him; but I arrived home late as I knew my Uncle was there and could help. When I came home, my Uncle had indeed taken Dad to the toilet and Dad whimpered to me,

"You said you'd be back to help me!"

It was with shame that I realised my failing. I had not provided the dignity that was so necessary to preserve for Dad at all costs.

A major question throughout this period was of how much was Dad aware? There was so much mental deterioration, that we were unsure at times as to his ability to respond to our reality. He was not talking by this point and the few attempts there were ended in frustration and tears, as he could not make himself understood. This was the situation I left as I went to college. Yet again I remained silent to most about the desperate pain of home.

Our local Doctor had told us that Dad must now be confined to hospital. This was an unacceptable and devastating thought, that Dad should be taken from us. Mum though as the primary carer was exhausted and desperately needed a respite. Dad did go into the local psychiatric ward for a week but was very disturbed by the whole experience. His only words on arriving home were, "I was misplaced."

It was this sense of being misplaced that was to continue, as no Doctors

were able to diagnose specifically what his needs were.
Mum and I began to talk openly during this time of Dad's death, as it was confirmed to us that he would deteriorate now until death. She asked me if I was angry with God? Internally I was raging, but on the outside clung onto a calm confused exterior.

It was coming to the end of term and Christmas was approaching. College had just been a place where I had existed. I did not feel that I belonged; my concerns were always focused towards my tormented home. I did not talk much to anyone, as I didn't want to expose my faltering faith amongst so many religious people.

I occasionally got asked by an innocent bystander if I was all right. I would always reply, "Yes, fine," so that this madness would not totally consume my life there as well. I pleaded with God to send me people with whom I could be honest, and a small network of friends developed who were to provide invaluable support. As I thought of home and the immanent Christmas festivities, I was aware that this was to be our last one together as a family. It's anticipation was loaded with emotion.

I was though not prepared for the acceleration of events on my return home. Dad was much worse physically. As he lay on his bed, his whole body shook to his sobs and cries of anguish. There was nothing to console with, and I just entered into his response. Dad had not passed urine for forty-eight hours and we had to take him to hospital for a catheter. His whining pierced the heart as he clung onto us, desperately grabbing for a hand. I have never seen a person so frightened and it was a terrifying experience.

During this final period of Dad's suffering I was aware that we were just waiting for him to die. I didn't know what to do, as it was a period of complete transition. Nobody wanted him to leave us and yet to watch his suffering was even worse. I have often thought of this time that having to live beside a man so ill and observe his sickness and helplessness, is almost as bad for those who watch as those who suffer.

I had unconsciously been praying for a long time that Dad may be allowed to die, to be removed from this undignified tormented state. Dad had now caught a cold and we could hear his continual spluttering, a sound that was to haunt me for the first few years after his death. I now knew that death was the only healing Dad was going to receive. I prayed for it with great pain. By now a care home had been suggested and rejected, as we the family, would look after him and surround him with the love he needed.

As Dad was now so ill, we had regular visits from a lovely District Nurse who did all she could to help Mum and make Dad comfortable in his distress. It was also during this time that a new minister at the church began to visit regularly, and offered the practical support that we so desperately needed. As a family we decided that we all wanted to attend church the following week, simply as a sign of need and solidarity.

The new assistant minister who began to come round and visit the family, was a gentle man who offered love and concern. We all grew to love him very much, as he administered Christ's healing presence to us. The most memorable occasion during this final period of Dad's life was a Communion we were all to share. We all gathered in our front room, the scene of the healing service all those years ago. As the minister, Mum and I began to say the liturgy we heard Dad's murmured tones. He was speaking coherently as we joined in the Lord's Prayer together. I can't express how powerful this was; that a man who had spoken no words in the previous months should now verbally enter into the mystery of the Eucharist.

Christmas Day came and went, but on Boxing Day I found Dad collapsed on his bedroom floor his face pressed into the carpet; we were both very distressed. In January the hospital informed us of what we already knew, he had no quality of life. I just wished for his humiliation to cease as it had gone on for far too long. Death was constantly in my thoughts by this point, but I was aware of how precious it was to be able to care for him.

The tension was enormous as I knew I was dying with him but still wanted to cling on, to try and create life in this desperate situation. I do not think I have prayed harder words than those asking Christ to receive Dad and give him release.

I was soon to return to college and felt strongly that I should begin to tell Dad how I loved and valued all that he had given and taught me. It was now a question of time, I returned the next evening and just lay down next to him. I told him that I knew his time was short. I just lay next to him in the darkness telling him how we all loved him.

As I held his hand his grip tightened to reassure me that he knew of my presence. We were silent for much of the time, but tears came as we just lay there anticipating his release. I cannot remember my exact words or for how long I spoke, but as I left Dad that night I knew it was the last intimate expression I would share alone until we met in Paradise. I wept as I thought of how special Dad had been, remained and would become.

The next day I returned to the seeming insanity of college life but remained in close contact with my family. The family now told me that the Doctor had said that time was short. I remained by the phone desperate and frantic every time it rang. Was it bringing news of Dad's death and would I ever see him again?

All of us knew that we could not be certain that we'd be there in Dad's last moments, but again there was something within that gave a certainty that I would see him before he died. It was the waiting which sapped the energy and emotion, we were entirely powerless to alter the course of events. The time was upon me when I could weep no more tears of anguish and pain at Dad's suffering. I wept now for my own personal loss of such a special father and friend.

I did not doubt God now, but had moved far from the image of Him as victoriously dynamic. Christian suffering was as painful as any other. I wondered what would happen to my own spirituality when Dad died; as he had been the focus of my life and attention for so long. I had a tremendous fear that I might cease to believe after Dad had gone. I did not know what I would do if this happened.

My family had found some comfort in my faith and yet I was experiencing an increasing alienation from it. There were now so many things of which I was unsure. I did not want to leave the security of faith that I had known, but I could no longer hold it in the context of my life experience. I did not reject God but needed to discover new ways to experience and understand Him.

One morning in the middle of a lecture, I suddenly decided to return home. I had already got a packed bag and I sat on the train returning to London. On the Tube I met a woman I knew who asked me how I was. I replied that I was returning home as I was unsure whether my father was dead or not.

Home was by now just a place of waiting, it was only a couple of days before Dad died. I can remember the scene vividly as my eldest sister and I sat on his bed and watched the sun gradually fade and the room darken. Dad's breathing was coming in gasps. We just sat in silence watching him go grey. He was quite cold by this time as all of his organs were ceasing to function. Neither of us moved. We were caught by the moment, transfixed by the sound of his breath.

Suddenly the door opened and Mum came in. Immediately I felt guilt at having been so selfish in not telling her of the developments; we left to give her the time she needed with the man she adored.

At five-thirty that evening, Dad died with his whole family around him. His mother was there, his wife, his five children and three grandchildren; all were there to pay tribute to a man much loved.

I felt nothing as I now had no father. I felt no alienation from God, as God didn't seem to matter anymore.

Chapter 7: 'A funeral and a Battle '

"Our grief is balanced by a recognition of Dad's salvation, the ambiguity of his plea for mercy, yet his acknowledgement of his future glory. Maybe it is our grace that Dad suffered no more pain but moved into the arms of God. Maybe it's only in the darkness of despair, that we can truly perceive the rays of hope and resurrection. There are many unanswered questions. As a family it would be naive to say that we have reconciled these with Dad's suffering; but we all recognise Gods grace, especially as we were all with Dad when he died."

As I spoke these words at the funeral there was a feeling that the only people who could speak about Dad were his family. We were the ones who had suffered so directly with him. We had cared and looked on at his last moments. As I looked around the church I saw so many people there from all of our lives. People of whom I knew nothing, people whom I would later discover had shared much with Mum and Dad in their previous life before me.

As we waited by the church entrance to thank people for coming, words of depth and understanding greeted us. I was dreading the final farewell, as we made our way to the crematorium. As I watched the coffin slide away from us, I let out a quiet yelp at this final and absolute departure. These were the first tears and Mum took my hand as we sang even louder to Wesley's 'Love Divine.'

As everyone left the house we were alone in our own silence, struck by our own personal pain. It was a pain that needed no explanation. No words could have expressed it, even if we had had the strength to try. An elder sister said to me; "You gave me hope today as I know now that Dad is at peace." Ironically it was this hope I myself was trying to cling on to.

I stayed at home for the first couple of weeks, desperately trying to avoid the familiar faces of the village. I then returned to what seemed my meaningless existence at college. I was met by a few excellent supportive friends, they did not ask the inane question of 'How are you feeling?' It was obvious that I was dying inside. I had lost everything, the man I loved so much and the faith I was brought up on.

It was terrifying to be thrown into the abyss of confusion and doubt. I wanted desperately to return to the certainties of my faith, and yet I knew that it had been destroyed. I was going to have to start again.

In those first few months I experienced constant dreams and whisperings about Dad's death. I would sit in lectures and hear his last gasps for breath. I would see his grey cold body, feel the lifeless corpse as I kissed him for the last time. I could not go to chapel, as to be with other people was an impossible thing.

I needed to be alone and would often take off early in the morning; as I knew it was going to be a bad day. It would be a day when I could think of nothing else but the father I'd lost. I would run out blind with tears onto the Downs passing people, who must have stared in amazement. I was only young, I should not lose my father at twenty; this is the age when he becomes your best friend, when you enter adulthood together.

At times I could sit in a pub totally detached from the conversation which surrounded me. On other occasions I would feel an anger welling up within me, aware of a violence which I had never previously known. It was at its worst when people were talking about God. I became highly judgmental and animated as I felt, 'You know nothing about God, suffering and life!' I had become baptised into the belief that suffering and death are the only true signs of integrity and life. Despair needed to be experienced before one could offer depth and wisdom; anything else was just superficial and meaningless.

I had little sympathy for people who were experiencing what I regarded as the 'normal' difficulties of life. My compassion was only aroused within a comparison to my own pain. I was so angry at times that I would have to get up and leave certain situations; occasions when trite platitudes were being shared about the 'meaning of life'. I felt I'd been betrayed by life and possibly God. I could not tolerate 'nice' Christian chat or indeed general pub talk. Everything was too intense for me. I was unable to enter into social situations without feeling in some way detached. Nothing was easy, simple or enjoyable, I became a disillusioned observer.

During this time I felt empty and had little recognition of Dad's salvation, I was just glad he was with God now; that was all. I wondered what would happen to my spirituality, as Dad had been the focus of my concern for so long. I struggled with an increasing guilt over my developing crisis of faith. I did not want to lose my church and doctrines, but it felt as if I was being forced out by my own experience. No-one ever told me that the questions of faith were so isolating. I had come from a background which had answers for everything. Now I was just left with my doubts and aching pain.

As I tried to pray, I felt God tell me to accept my pain and crisis before Him. I had a confused spirituality which was accusing me of my doubts. My prayer during this time was that I might be allowed to have the time and space to be angry. I hoped that if this was possible I would find God again. This was a period when I sought solitude, I did not want the advice of others, as I knew that I must work this out alone before God. I found college unbearable with its claustrophobic concerns. It became a prison for me from which I needed to escape.

Frequently, I sat alone and wept. I realised that crying was an opportunity to release the moments, hours, days, weeks and years of relentless pain in a few precious moments. It was a period of absolute isolation.

All my family were experiencing their own tremendous grief, and were consequently unable to respond to mine. It was not that we were unaware of each other, it was just impossible to move beyond the walls of grief which surrounded each of us. I remember a walk on the Downs when I was blinded by my own tears. I felt that no one could possibly understand, as I considered the meaningless existence I now possessed.

It was the first time that I had fully acknowledged that I did not want to live; of course the feeling was always around, but this was the point of decision. I did walk to the Gorge and speculate about ending my life. It was not a moment of hysterical tension, but an appraisal of what would happen. As I thought about this, I was reminded of my promise to Dad that we would look after Mum. I knew I could do no more to harm her so I walked away that day from my possible escape, back into the arms of chaos.

As I tried to pray I became more confused through my anger at God and the church, as my isolation was so terrible. I needed to search for God in the pain. It was necessary for me to retreat from the world at this time, as I knew that there were no adequate responses for me. I was also aware that if I sought answers from others, my very passion and intensity would destroy them. It was almost as if I was looking for safety measures for preservation of self and others. I needed to build a fence around me. To protect myself from people's potential insensitivity, as well as to protect them from my ferocious anger.

As I began to wrestle with the pain of Dad's experience, I sought the beginnings of a new spiritual framework. I wanted to challenge the insensitivity that my family had experienced. I was desperate to discover a God of compassion, a true belief in which I would find that those who suffered belonged to God. Rejection was our human experience, but I could not believe that we were forsaken by God.

As I continued to think about health and healing in the light of my own experience. I began to recognise that the fundamental question I was asking was; What makes for healing?

As I pursued this I began to recognise that I had moved far from the belief that healing was a person's right; as so often it could not be achieved or given. I began to understand healing to be the desire to see the priceless human being, within the frail broken earthen vessel.

I had heard so many people say of their own pain, “It's not fair! Why me?” I was beginning to learn the hard answer to this question. “Why not you?” None of us can build protective walls around ourselves which are impenetrable.

Pain was a familiar companion and yet the burden had become too heavy. My relief during this time was to begin marking up my pain points and giving myself a life score. I would sit in a cynical corner muttering about the injustice of it all. Daring others to challenge me, and accusing all who had not suffered. It was at times a satisfying place, almost a pseudo enlightenment. I now knew that life was about suffering. I had learnt the hardest lesson at an early age. Life is hard. Now I could at least take the opportunity to inform others of what was coming to them.

Friendship did once again distract me for a while as I established close companionship with a few. It provided a breathing space, an opportunity for tears and laughter. Pain though sought this out, as a close friend expressed her desire to become lovers. This natural and normal progression of emotions took me entirely by surprise. I was totally naive to the needs of others, and the depth of emotional links I had demanded and created.

It was with neurotic fury that I denied this friend any possibility of love and further friendship. I had not asked for anything more, nor did I want it. I was terrified that this inner sanctum of peace and freedom should be violated in this way. I reacted as one who knew violation and previous abuse, and sensed it again. Irrationally I lashed out, frightened and sometimes unaware to the depth of my emotions. My only rational during this time was that I had not asked for this expression of love, therefore it should not confront me. I did not make links back to my earlier experiences. I simply lashed out with the strength of a boy who was now a man.

It was only in my next and later relationship that I began to admit to some of my tremendous need and neurosis. Driven once again by an adolescent desire to belong I embraced another wounded lover with the intensity of life itself; and for a while we touched.

It was though during the intensity of this embrace that the pain began to re-emerge within crushing emotional need. This need to make all things safe and certain in an attempt to at last belong. I could not see or admit this at the time, the destructive quality of these emotions that kept driving me forward. It was fear of further loss which fuelled this whole episode, and propelled me towards the abyss of having to let go.

I had in this final year of college become more aloof, and was set up for that classic inabesentia student degree. I was finding increasing difficulty in the idea of being a friendly parish priest. As I wanted to tear the world apart. I was not conscious about that which prompted my next decision, but I knew that I could not simply leave college and step into a parish. It appears strange to me now that I shouldn't have realised my whole being was screaming in protest at the idea of becoming a priest; to become like those who had hurt and abused me.

Clear insight was not though readily available, so I just went with my gut which mumbled that now was possibly not the best time to take on a responsible and significant community role. All was then agreed. I was to leave college with my theology degree, splattering of Greek, commitment to justice, overdraft and seething anger.

I arrived in East London full of naiveté and romantic vision. I wanted to do some real work in the inner-city, to knock out some of my middle-class guilt and privilege. To become a 'real person' in a world I'd never previously encountered.

There is always a great humour about those of us who come to save. This is that we are generally blissfully ignorant of our own need of saving. This is God's humour not mine. That I should be saved by my desire to help those that I perceived as vulnerable, had something to do with a speck and a beam. My salvation was to be discovered in the Franciscan colour brown and a challenging and turbulent work experience.

I began work in Tower Hamlets in a long established temperance mission, whose focus was to help those with addiction based problems. It was a sobering experience.

I must admit that a part of my reason for coming to this new situation, was because I knew that counselling would be offered as a part of my work supervision. I longed for the opportunity to simply let go of all of the pain which was knotted and twisting around inside of me. I had become bored by my own angry story. I no longer quite believed it, and certainly did not know how to end it.

On reflection it's not so strange that I choose to begin my place of healing within an organisation which had strong similarities to the church I had grown up in. Maybe deep down I knew that I had to face the phantoms and dragons again. Alternatively, it could perhaps be better viewed as simply, clever old God.

It was a strange sequence of events which were to develop over a period of just under two years, during which I was a part of this organisation. It was a mixed relationship of powerful contradictions. I wanted to belong but fought desperately against the subtle and blatant demands of this group.

It was an organisation which aimed to live as a lay community. A group of genuinely committed people, seeking to live a generous life in the service of others. It was an attractive ideal, offering the potential to live in a way which would respond to the altruism and faith within.

My experience was though from the beginning an uncomfortable one. There was something familiar about the characters and the role I was playing. There were people who knew pain, and others who remained unscathed by life. I just couldn't discover where it was that I was to fit in.

My role became apparent as time went on. I was a peripheral member, someone who was not felt to be as committed as the rest. A person who was just passing through. It was a familiar place but I found some worthy companions.

As I began my soul searching I was told of my tremendous anger and grief. It was I must admit not a surprise, ironically rather a relief. At last, I had found a 'counsellor' within supervision who would take on my pain.

It was a long and difficult process. The necessity for life stories, for intricate details to be drawn and relived from my past. It felt at times self-obsessed and frantic; but I was desperate to take this, any opportunity, to expiate the raging pain of the past.

It took about a year to come to a place of letting go of my grief. It was also the beginning of crying myself to sleep, waking up in tears and experiencing panic attacks. Letting go was terrifying. Especially of the protective shield behind which I often hid. Grief had been an offensive weapon which had served me so well in the height of battle and rage. I did though let go and seek to live in a way which was not driven by the past loss of a father.

It was a hard thing to accept that I was fatherless.

The bitter blow was not in this realisation, but through what the acceptance and letting go enabled to surface. Abuse was to become the word and memory raging around my head for the next eighteen months.

When I first told my Counsellor about the story of abuse I was unimpassioned. It was just another link in the chain, a part of my history. A reason for childhood resentment towards the church I grew up in. It was though the Counsellor's response which allowed me the first glimpse and possibility, that my experience had been as terrible as I had known it. One of the first things which confronts an adult ten years on from abuse is the question; Was it really true? There is a very rational reason for this. An adult mind assumes that if it was really that traumatic you would have done something about it. A great tragedy and failing of my recall was that the events never felt as terrible and destructive as they did as a child. My biggest challenge at this point was whether I was to take myself seriously.

One of the ways in which the issue gained momentum was that this group of people with whom I worked, rightly commented that I was always an outsider. They wanted me to belong, to draw me into the group. To offer me acceptance. I think it was at this point that I knew that this would never be possible. A fundamental point was that I had never belonged anywhere. It was not a choice I was at liberty to make, it was an impossible request and one which signalled my departure.

The advantage of hindsight, (and good therapy!), allows me to see that I had chosen as my place for healing a situation which was familiar to my past. It was a group of enthusiastic Christian people who were led by a strong charismatic figure. It was potentially a place for ideals. At worse a place of dependence.

The familiar echo of 'You are angry' and 'You need to let go' cashed in on emotions which were deeply entrenched. I did not need to be told how I was feeling. I wanted to be offered a way out. It was strange that at my time of deepest need and crisis, my work supervisor and counsellor told me to stop being angry with him. It was a complete denial of all that I needed to be. He had set himself up as a person of trust and significance, but like the previous adults who encountered me; denied me part of my story. He could not cope with the anger and confusion of relationships within a working environment. It became evident that we were a threat to one another, and I began to withdraw from the therapeutic process with a question. Why should he be allowed power and insight, if he was not prepared to equally make himself vulnerable with another?

My active and positive choice within this was to find a therapist who was neither male or Christian. It was a progressive moving away from this Christian group who sought to heal through the offer of belonging; without even asking if I wanted to belong. My experience was that this group was far from accepting when I chose to move outside of their juristriction. It was the same voice in the present which said 'You can belong' as had told me in the past, that I could also belong to a charismatic movement. Neither voices I felt fully understood themselves, or knew of what they were a part. Subsequently they could not make me a genuine offer.

It was a strange experience to try to belong for a period to a group which could never have offered me a home. It was though an important time; as despite the inevitable explosions and accusation, I moved on and away with a deep sense of integrity and personal joy. Second time around I had understood the group I was a part of, and made the right choice to depart. It was a lesson which had at last been learnt. I no longer needed to return to particular charismatic Christians. At last I knew as an adult what I couldn't have learnt as a child. I did not want to belong, because I did not belong. I had the power of choice as an adult, an opportunity often denied a child.

It may seem obvious, but it was only in moving from this tight-knit community which had rightly pointed out and observed my pain; that I was in a position to deal with it.

I remember sitting down talking to my new therapist, deeply relieved that she was without the church. There was no pressure or threat. No confused roles or relationships, just a person who would sit and listen to me.

Chapter 8: 'The Past and the Present'

My interactions with my Mum were approached through a ruthless honesty. This becoming the foundation on which our relationship became reforged. My request was that she was not to feel that she should try and hold me in places, which had previously been the realm of father and son. This was to create a genuine place of freedom. It was an honesty which allowed the basis for the final exorcism to take place.

As I became fully aware of the pain I felt through the experience of abuse and betrayal, I knew that whatever actions I would take would also be costly to my family; particularly Mum. She was still living in the family home on her own, surrounded by many of the people who had been my tormentors. There was something perverse within this sudden awareness on my part, about the feelings of these 'others'. My real immediate need and desire was to shout out my real story, without reserve and concern for potential pain and embarrassment for others. I chose though to show restraint, in an attempt to protect those who had so generously cared for me in the past.

If I was to try and describe my Mum the word most often given by others of her; this is that she is a lady. This is not a prissy or politically incorrect description, but a word charged with tremendous power. It speaks of her great inner courage and commitment at caring for a husband and family. It also tells of her choice to continue to believe despite all circumstances.

It was into my Mum's arms that I cried, when I first realised the extent and devastation of the abuse and betrayal. It was then to her that I returned, as I spoke of my desire to take this matter up with the diocese. I knew that the cost to her would be high as she was still a member of the local church, which she'd attended for thirty years. It was a small community in which she lived. Mum then risked far more exposure than I, with my anger and anonymity in London.

Abuse is a very disabling experience as it disconnects you from yourself, from others and from the past. It was for me an unknown experience which was only now finding a voice and the possibility of articulation. It was not a dramatic or hysterical realisation of past hurt, but rather a self awakening, an explanation for present attitudes and behaviour. Only at this point was I able to link the huge conflict for me with my movement towards the church. This was not an immediate insight but a gradual awareness which allowed me to discuss my experience.

It is often the case that the abused of any description, are already vulnerable and susceptible to further betrayal. This had certainly been my experience as a teenager desperate for stability and belonging. As an adult I clearly remembered that I had already stood at the gate of many an adult conversation, desperately wanting to be let in. It was though the two contradictory forms of adult acceptance which had been so confusing during this period. One man had loved and cared for me, but was told to go away because the church did not like him. The other man came from within the church, groped and trapped me; this time I was told to leave.

A period of eighteen months began in which I began to retell my story before attentive, distracted and uncaring listeners. It was a time when I wanted to run through the streets of my home town, to re-visit all of my school friends. To tell the story which had never been told, to speak the names of those involved.

It was a period of many meetings, phatasisical and real. I can remember sitting with close friends discussing the possibility of public media exposure. I recall hearing a Bishop and close clergy friends speak of the need to exorcise the ghosts of the past, to make the church a place of truth.

I experienced the rage of sisters who wanted to get on a plane and find this priest, to tell him of their necessary defence of their brother through his growing up; in an often hostile and unforgiving environment. I felt too my own confused cry of anger and pain. I felt too that my family needed to receive recognition from the church as to the pain that they saw me go through; as well as that which they personally encountered. There was an anger on my part, that my parents hospitality should have been abused in this way. This priest was a guest in their home at the request of the church.

Maybe it is because I am not a SUN newspaper reader, that I ultimately felt that media attention was not the best way forward. There was much of it around at this time with similar types of cases. Or maybe there was something within me which did not want God shamed anymore then the church had already done. You see it had never ultimately been an issue about God and me, it was simply a conflict with those who represented him.

I have always strongly believed that my experience and faith in God was maintained, solely because the church did not have ownership of him.

It was the sense that God lived, breathed and loved outside of the church. This became the foundation stone for my re-creation of faith.

A considerable conflict though remained. I wanted to belong to the church. Not because I felt I needed too; but because I felt that at best the church was a true glimpse of community, belonging and relationship. I wanted to set myself free from this previous violation, free to choose whether to stay or go.

Resolution however was to be a very long and complex process, as I began a conversation with the institution of the church. I wrote my first letter to a contact I had within the diocese. In it I expressed my awareness of the enormity of what I was now saying ten years later. I stated that it had only been because of my Dad's continual illness and death, that the abuse registered as insignificant in comparison to the man I loved so much. I expressed my fear at what this procedure might entail.

This dialogue with the wider church was sometimes confused, often angry, but always concerned. I was so grateful for the initial response I received; it was so evident that I had been BELIEVED. It was the permission to remember, to really try and heal the wound.

I can remember while I was at college trying to respond to the mass of anger within. I was nicknamed as the man who knew 'where he didn't come from'. Such was my antagonism and feeling to my home church. I was so able to state what I was not, but struggled to indicate what I was, or wanted to become.

It was while I was at college I clearly remembered being frightened by a tremendous power and anger. I knew I did not control it yet, therefore it terrified me with its outbursts and judgements. An attempt to absolve this pain was to write during this period to my original church leaders. In doing this I shared my sense of guilt and shame at being angry with them, over what I understood at the time to be an issue of mis-placed grief.

I do not then remember a time when I didn't want to finish and resolve this pain.

As my dialogue continued with the church, there was a growing awareness on my part that I had taken a considerable risk in once again trusting an institution, which had in the past been the context for so much past failing. Silence became increasingly unnerving during a period of emotional turbulence. I felt very alone and in awe of the church, swaying between extreme anger and a sense of defeat.

A part of my difficulty was that I was now talking with the immediate family about all of these issues and their experience. All of these factors created a high level of emotional exhaustion and anxiety. On occasions I wanted to return to my home church and confront them with their failing. I wanted them to personally acknowledge the tremendous battle which raged at times, as I tried to hold onto self belief. I had spent a life time trying to justify inconsistencies and wrong doing by the church I grew up in. All I was now left with was a sensation that it was probably all my fault.

My first disappointment came when the diocesan Bishop expressed extreme dismay over the way my family and I had been treated. The sting in the tail was though that he indicated that he had no authority over the church in question. He could inform them of my complaint and add his own grievance at their misconduct. It was though a question of that particular churches clergy's integrity.

The Bishop's comment at this point was that he was not very hopeful that they would make an adequate response. My reply was to say that I realised this, but I felt a need to at least make them aware of their failing. I knew that my resolve was not going to be dependent upon these local clergy's response. I would not give them that much power.

I left the Bishop glad of his empathy, but disappointed at his lack of authority.

My major concern after this meeting was to discover where Bill the priest who had abused me, was living. I had a sick gut reaction that he was likely to be abusing others. I felt a tremendous responsibility to prevent any further pain caused by his perversion. It took some time but I eventually tracked down the priest, only to discover that he had died of malaria a year earlier. It was devastating. I was denied the chance of communicating with my oppressor. If I had followed the earlier intention of my twin sister, we would have flown to Bill's home and confronted him ourselves.

What became strange was that my rage was no longer focused solely with this man, but with those who had condoned his behaviour. It does not mean that I would have been civil with Bill, had I met him, but he was certainly only a part of the equation.

To be honest I felt the next stage was predictable. I sensed the church at a diocesan level breathe a huge sigh of relief. There could be no substantial scandal now, as the man in question was dead; consequently there was damage limitation. As the wheels of motion gained some momentum, I was aware of a considerable split within the church that I knew.

I had tremendous support from another Bishop, a Franciscan Brother, and various priests and friends, telling me that I must make choices for myself. To exorcise this experience from my past. They told me that the church must be made accountable, otherwise it could not stand for truth. On the other hand I was aware of a growing feeling that the issue was beginning to resolve and naturally diffuse itself, through my own growing awareness and actions.

The reality of this change became apparent when a meeting was arranged for my sister and I, to meet with the two clergy relating to the adolescent experience. The anticipation was terrible, and I was off work for a two days trying to prepare myself. It was an opportunity in which I believed so much from the past could find a resolve. I approached it then with optimism and fear. I did not have much faith in the two clergymen, but a basic understanding and apology was all I wanted. Five minutes would have been enough. I still wanted to believe in these people, to complete this whole episode.

To say that the meeting was a disaster could only really be fully possible if I had a transcript of the dialogue. It began by the Vicar of the church I had grown up in asking why he was at this meeting. This was despite phone calls and specific correspondence from me and the diocese relating to this whole episode of abuse. It was then with some confusion and hurt that I retorted, we were here to deal with my experience within his church.

No doubt the meeting was a failure from the point that this Vicar and his colleague chose not to read the extensive correspondence which was sent them; or to extend the basic human expression of respect. It was an abortive time in which the colleague who had so curtly dismissed me in my youth remained silent, as he carefully studied the pattern of the carpet. The Vicar expressed little, except that maybe I was overreacting to my experience; he then offered to pay for some counselling I was having.

Apart from not wanting the thirty pieces of silver, I took the opportunity to view two men from my new perspective as an adult. They had spent their entire ministries speaking of love and healing, yet clearly in this instance lacked any courage to even listen to the experience and existence of pain.

It took considerable time to get over this encounter which the Bishop's assistant acknowledged was a disaster. It remained though my desire to pursue the possibility of resolve and limited reconciliation. More letters were then written and a final meeting was arranged with just the Vicar, the Bishop's assistant, my sister and Mum. I included my Mum as I felt she was certainly due an apology for her experience as a parent and church member.

Extreme pastoral ineptitude is the only appropriate description of this last and final encounter. We were led by the Vicar into a small upper room which was used by a children's group. It was furnished only by two old sofas with throw over blankets. I was embarrassed not simply by the environment, but by the Vicar's opening remark.

"So what are we here for then Jeremy: Is it to kiss, cuddle and make up?"

It was an extraordinary introduction which led only to a predictable denial of any accountability. It was deja vu in which I now heard as an adult ten years on, exactly what I had heard as a teenager. I was basically told that my experience was exaggerated, and that the priest who abused me would have brought this local church into disrepute. The Vicar said that he had in fact written to the priest in question, and told him he was never again welcome in his parish. Though he promised this to my parents, it's ironic that even this small gesture was never relayed back to me at the time.

In many ways it was a completely surreal experience as my worst fantasy had come true, in terms of an awful conclusion from the local church to my painful experience. It was though in real terms, a truly liberating time as the teenager within me was at last validated and believed by me as an adult. I had heard exactly the same excuses and fumblings ten years on.

The difference was that now as an informed adult I knew my experience to be true. The vicar was a man who had spoken to me of freedom and healing in my youth, who could not even see the blockage and time bomb he had placed in another's life.

I was able to leave that meeting with my Mum and sister at last liberated. We had the unspoken acknowledgement from the Bishop's assistant of this Vicar's considerable failing; but much more importantly our own experience. Liberation is found in the strangest places but I can honestly say that mine came with a clear adult realisation and acceptance of this local churches failing to me and my family.

Chapter 9: 'Chasing Spirituality'

Letting go is a long and painful process. It is spoken of often within therapeutic and spiritual climates. It is believed to be the 'right thing' to enable growth, life and new possibilities. Letting go was a nightmare.

It was not about a recognised and identifiable process. It was not about something clean, thorough and obvious. It involved bitterness, pain and resentment. It embraced familiar patterns, judgements and relationships. Letting go was not simply common sense. Letting go for me was about a changing of attitude within a pressing need.

Something deep happened within me when I returned to those who had hurt me. It was in many ways a naming of the anger, a facing of the enemy. My tormentors when approached were not in fact as powerful or threatening as I feared. They were basically men who remained unaware to the extent to which they had damaged me. It was not necessarily a deliberate or conscious act which had maimed me; simply a culture and belief system which had not been able to embrace pain.

There remains within me an angry disillusioned teenager who wants to still shout about the remaining injustices and failings of some church leaders, who fail to engage with the disaffected of life. It is much simpler for these people to avoid truth by an excersion of their power, by using avoidance and exclusion. It would have been easy to write a book specifically about this type of failing, because it has been so significant within my experience. I do not though believe that I would have offered very much; except maybe the opportunity for the maimed and disaffected to gather around and say 'Yes'.

The challenge though has always been bigger than this. It has been within me since I was conceived and is central to humanness. This is the desire to belong. Letting go is a process which finds itself deeply rooted in the attitude, that an awareness of personal pain is never enough.

There have been many people who have travelled with me who have offered great insight and compassion. Their love expressed itself in the challenge that there was the possibility of moving on.

Moving on was often an event in which I engaged without awareness. On other occasions it was a bloody battle in which the demands and cost were obvious. I can recall the inner turmoil and fear at not knowing how I was going to be when I woke up the next day. Would I want people around me, as I tried to confront myself and the pain I carried?

The institutional church was not always helpful. I am glad though that I always understood my healing was from a God who existed in his world, which was beyond the restrictions of religion and procedure. If this is a spiritual book it is only because it is an uncomfortable human story, in which God meets a person, amidst his turmoil, pain and suffering.

My challenge to move on has been based around the belief in the eternal. Grief, loss, abuse, betrayal are all part of the human story; but the possibility of eternity lives alongside them. It is not present in the sense of avoidance or denial; but expressed in a full and thorough confrontation of the pain. I could not have let go of past experience if I did not believe that there might be something to move onto.

There is I believe a part in all human experience which screams that this can not be all. It is resilient, provocative, challenging and intimately connected to God; because within the scream is often the desire to belong, to connect, to embrace.

I didn't always recognise this within myself, as anger and distrust are powerful barriers. Ultimately though they are not a point of denial, but a part of the process; as how can you truly dismiss eternity?

My journey has brought me back to the church through the friendship and care of many within and outside of it. I have been allowed to express my dis-connectedness, alongside my desire to belong. It has been a very powerful and helpful experience, to stand and shout outside the walls of the city. To scream of the hypocrisy and dis-satisfaction. The joke is though that when you are hoarse, and don't even remember what it is that you are now shouting about; you can often catch the small voice of love which offers the possibility of acceptance and belonging.

Sometimes the noise is too great and the satisfaction too much, to stop and listen to this voice. On other occasions the isolation is too familiar and reassuring that belonging seems almost insulting.

I stood on the outside for a very long time. Sometimes through choice and on occasion because I was forced there. It was at times a home. The irony was though that I actually wanted to go into the city, even though it may no longer be my home. I did make the decision to return to an institution which is both daunting and crumbling. Both challenging and irrelevant. I went because I wanted to belong in a fuller sense to myself and others, because I now knew why I had returned. It was because I had been listened too, and the previous pain didn't seem to matter anymore.

Postscript. 'Revisiting the Challenge'

I am free as I no longer need to talk about my pain. This freedom has come after long years of struggle. There has been no avoidance just periods of resting as the journey has been tough. The shouting has stopped as I know I have now been listened to. Being heard was all I wanted. To be believed, was the gift I found in the commitment of others.

I do not think of this as a sad story. It is simply an experience of life. It has held much pain, but has also allowed me to love and be loved deeply.

There have been many redeeming figures discovered inside and outside of the church. The lesson I have learnt, is that these figures within the church have often told me to seek out the people of faith outside of the institution. I am now free to return to the institution as the obstacles have at last been removed. It was the dedication and vulnerability of those helpers within the church, which gave me a genuine possibility of relating once more to the public face of faith.

I finish then by thanking all of those people who have allowed me to look beyond my own pain. They have revealed the possibility of living again. No doubt the beginning of a resurrection experience ....

What is I.C.C.S?

International:
We have teaching commitments in five large cities in the USA, as well as contacts in Canada and Sweden. We design one to three day workshops around the needs of specialised groups such as teachers, nurses, clergy, doctors, police, social workers, or anyone in the caring professions.

Communication:
The heart of I.C.C.S is in the field of communication. We live in an age of global communication but often when it comes to personal relationships, working with others and sharing our feelings openly many people find communication painfully difficult. We aim to improve communication on all levels, but beginning with oneself.

Counselling:
Over 50% of our time is spend with individual therapy and counselling. We offer a wide range of both pastoral counselling and psychotherapy. This includes Marriage and divorce counselling, psycho-sexual problems, bereavement, sexual and physical abuse, stress and career changes. We also offer supervision for professionals.

Skills:
Many of our training days involve the development and improvement of basic communication skills. These include 'Counselling in Cancer Care', 'Breaking Sad News to People', 'Basic Counselling Skills' and 'Marriage Preparation'.

I.C.C.S has published a number of books around the area of personal growth and development. All are available by contacting the office.

If you would like any further information on the wide range of teaching and counselling services that I.C.C.S offers, please contact Doug Hiza or Muriel Huntley on **0171 336 6197**.